STEP OUT FROM THE SHADOWS

"How to be seen and heard at work"

Sally Hindmarch

Publishing in the United Kingdom by: Sally Hindmarch

Cartoons created by: Stephanie Smith, Leamington Spa

Book design & layout by Velin@Perseus-Design.com

ISBN Number: 978-1-64713-109-8 (Paperback)

To Mum, Rob, Emily & Amy without whom everything would be in shadow;
and in memory of Dad who never got to write his book.

Table of Contents

Foreword

Step up! Be assertive! Don't let them walk all over you! You give the presentation! Tell them we're not happy!

These and so many other instructions issued (often well-meaningly) by bosses, friends and colleagues - but - missing that vital piece - how?

How do I step up? How do I become assertive without being blunt? What do I include in my presentation? How do I control those annoying 'nerves'?

Well, the answers to these and many, many other questions are answered by communications expert, Sally Hindmarch, in this, her insightful book, **Step Out from the Shadows**.

I first met Sally 6 years ago and immediately we connected. (How to do that is just one of the many ideas and proven methods Sally explains for you).

Since then we've spent more than 40 days together at various events and meetings and at every one I've learned more from her.

The one that resonates so strongly is her tripod/string/bolero process. That made me far more aware than ever before. I know you'll use it the moment you read the idea.

This short but jam-packed book is a compendium of ideas to get you more connected with yourself and others. The methods make you more aware of the words we say (internally and externally) and how we influence others to agree with our ideas in a structured and integrity-laden way.

If you want to increase your personal power, improve your communications skills (Check out Sally's L.U.C.I.D. method) or even stand and speak with power in front of others - then you're holding in your hand, right now, all the ideas you need to get there.

I wish you every success in the adventure with Sally as your guide

Peter Thomson
"The UK's Most Prolific Information Product Creator"
www.peterthomson.com

CHAPTER 1

A moment in my life

As I walked into my new office, on that cold Monday morning, I realised there was only a tiny corner where I wasn't visible, through the internal windows, to everyone else in the main open-plan office. I shut the office door and manoeuvred myself so I couldn't be seen. Taking deep breaths to try to stop my heart leaping out of my chest, I asked myself … "Oh God, what have I done?"

At that moment I knew I wasn't prepared … I wasn't ready and I wasn't experienced enough to be doing the job I had been given. The previous

Friday I had left my desk in the open-plan office and today I was in the corner office. I knew nothing had changed over the weekend and any minute now someone would notice.

Of course, I looked the part …

Navy suit, heels and jewellery. The visit to the hairdresser meant I looked like a senior manager and my makeup was neutral but sufficient. My daughter had drawn me a picture for my new office and I had a new notebook and pen. But that wasn't going to fool anybody; and the throbbing noise in my ears was getting louder.

I knew that outside there were people who wanted to know what to do and were waiting for me to make decisions. Decisions about what to do next, how they were to spend their time and how to handle clients, staff and suppliers. And I didn't know the answers … I didn't know what I was doing and any minute now everyone would realise I had no clue too.

After what felt like hours of my considering the easiest route out of the building and to the job centre there was a knock on the door and one of the team came into the office. Hurriedly I turned to the filing cabinet hoping she would think I was busy and looked round with a smile.

I can't remember what her question was but I remember I had to move to my desk. We spoke for a minute or two and she left with an answer … she hadn't laughed at me nor told me she knew I was a fraud. She thought I knew what I was doing … just as I had thought my managers had known what they were doing … and we were both wrong.

What I realised then …

And have proved to myself over and over again, is that most of us are just one step from being found out; we build on our experience and expertise hoping each time that this will help us do a better job. My managers hadn't known it all; they were trying their best, just as I was. When they had asked me for my thoughts it wasn't necessarily because they were leading me to an answer; it was probably because they didn't know the answer and were hoping I could come up with something instead, or at least give them time to think of something to say.

That was over twenty years ago but I haven't forgotten that moment.

I have got used to the feeling of not being entirely confident … I now recognise it as the precursor of great opportunities to come. The feeling of fear and excitement are the same, it is just what you label them that makes the outcome different.

Since that moment …

In my blue suit and corner office I have changed jobs, started businesses, closed businesses and I am still taking on projects that make my heart pound and my breath quicken. Writing this book is one of them!

In that time, I have worked with amazing people who have taught me (not always intentionally) how to have more impact on others and influence their actions by my choices. I have spent over fifteen years working with my team of professional actors at 'Partners With You'[1] who have taught me their techniques to look and sound more confident.

---

[1] www.partnerswithyou.co.uk

And I have trained with Prism Brain Mapping[2], Dr Maria Paviour[3] and Dr Lynda Shaw[4]; all working in the field of Neuroscience, to better understand what is actually going on in our brains and how to affect our behaviours and reactions.

Combined with this I have a lifetime of clients and colleagues who have taught me as much as I have been able to show them and of course the myriad of people whose paths have crossed mine. And to all of them I am grateful.

This book is an amalgamation of everything I have learnt.

My take on what I have seen, done, learnt and heard and all that entails. I will share insights into effective communication and give you the techniques that I and my clients have found most useful.

My aim is to give you the tools you need to be able to stand up and speak out on every occasion you choose to, knowing that you have presented the best version of you. Whatever your role, wherever you are in your career and whatever your reason for picking up this book my hope is that you will finish with a better understanding of how you can have impact and influence even when your heart is pumping and you don't believe that you can!

[2] www.prismbrainmapping.com

[3] www.mariapaviour.com

[4] www.drlyndashaw.com

CHAPTER 2

Managing & communicating with yourself

It might seem a little strange to start a book about how to better communicate with others by writing a chapter about communicating with yourself, but, bear with me. In the next few pages I'm going to talk about two areas that I think are crucial to being able to communicate well. How to feel comfortable being you and how to stop yourself from undermining your own authority.

So, first of all …

Can you hear that?

Listen carefully … can you hear it? …

What?

That voice in your head which, right now, is probably saying something like "Hear what?", "What am I meant to be able to hear?"

Everyone has one, for some it is louder than for others but we all have this voice giving us a running commentary on what we are doing and how well we are doing it. Many tell me that their internal voice talks to them constantly and this voice is really harsh. This voice can say things to you that you would never say to other people. It can negate, fat shame, deride and much more, generally making you feel less than you are.

That was the voice that was telling me I wasn't up to it as I stood hidden in my new corner office. It's the one that questions my decisions and has me second guessing what someone really meant by a particular turn of phrase or comment.

How do you stop it?

Well my first tip is to give it a name. By disassociating yourself from the voice you can start to discuss, disagree and ignore the comments. I've found that just splitting myself from this voice has allowed me to acknowledge that it is there, that it has my back and is trying to keep me safe, but that I don't need the advice right now! My name for mine is Great Aunt Gertie and she is a stickler for manners and behaviour. She tells me that I am an idiot; frequently and has very high standards! She also assumes I can't do whatever it is I am thinking about doing as her starting point.

Yours may not be quite as negative, but it probably is. When I talk about this negative voice most people know what I am talking about. They recognise the inner gremlin who tries to stop us from being hurt. And that is what it is, it's just our brains trying to stop us from coming to harm. If you consider that your brain's function is to keep you safe and alive then it isn't surprising that your version of Great Aunt Gertie might try to stop you from doing anything that could possibly put you at risk.

And remember that for most people, the risks we take aren't really life threatening. But Great Aunt Gertie doesn't necessarily know that. For example; you are waiting at the side of a stage about to walk on to present. You start to feel butterflies in your stomach, you get short of breath, your heart beats faster and your hands become clammy. Your sympathetic nervous system is kicking into gear to get your body ready for fighting or fleeing. Your inner voice starts telling you to get out of there.

Now, imagine you are in a dark room, the lights have gone out and you hear a gunshot from outside … same feelings, same inner voice telling you to get out of there. In both instances the same reaction, both to try to save you. But at the side of the stage you don't need to fight or flee, your life isn't really in danger but your version of Great Aunt Gertie doesn't know that.

So, in that moment …

You need to start conversing with your inner gremlin. Thank them for their comments and then tell them that you don't need to worry at the moment as you are excited to be going on stage. Remember, those butterflies and a faster beating heart are also the signs of being super excited … just because Great Aunt Gertie says you are scared, doesn't mean you have to be. You have the choice to disagree.

As well as reacting to your inner gremlin you can start doing some "seven-eleven" breathing. My colleague Annie Farr taught me this and it has been a life saver for me (or at least has saved me from drying up mid-sentence with a microphone in my hand).

"Seven-Eleven" Breathing

Breath in deeply for the count of seven and then out for the count of eleven. Close your eyes if you can and just concentrate on breathing in as you count to seven and out as you count to eleven. Do this 3 or 4 times and you will start to feel calmer.

When your sympathetic nervous system kicks in you are getting ready to fight or flee so your heartbeat accelerates to pump blood and your body readies itself to run or move quickly. In contrast your parasympathetic nervous system works to calm you down and allow you to rest. Both of these are automatic (subconscious) responses and by breathing to seven-eleven you trigger the 'calming down' response.

At its simplest …

If you were in danger you wouldn't breathe deeply, consequently, if you are breathing deeply you can't be in danger and your body will react accordingly.

If you find that seven-eleven breathing is too hard, try counting in for five and out for nine instead. The important thing is to count and breath out for longer than your breath in.

I said earlier that we tend to speak to ourselves much more harshly than we ever would anyone else. I wouldn't dream of saying the things I say to myself, to others. I wouldn't, for example, tell a friend of mine that I think her outfit is dreadful and she has no taste … and yet I (or Great Aunt Gertie) has said that and a lot more.

Start to notice what you are saying …

And how you are describing yourself in a situation. When you are berating yourself would you say "I am an idiot*" or "I am behaving like an idiot*"? (*Feel free to insert a word that you criticise yourself with rather than the one Great Aunt Gertie prefers!)

When you describe *yourself* as an idiot there is nowhere to go. It has a permanence. When you describe your *behaviour* as idiotic there is room for change, development and growth. This is important because what we tell ourselves is what we tell others.

I have a client (let's call her Jane) who says things during her presentations like – "I'm no expert" and "I'm sure I'm not right" and "I don't really know anything about this". When Jane and I started working together I asked her why she said these things. Her response was "I don't want anyone to think

I know more than I do" and "It's better to tell people I know I'm no good rather than them working it out for themselves". During the conversation Jane made more disparaging remarks about herself and I set her the job of noticing what she said to herself for a week.

The results were (unsurprisingly) that she usually started her statements with "I am" and she had grown to believe that this was a truth about herself. Over time Jane began to correct herself so she would change the internal comment from "I am stupid" to "That was stupid" or "I behaved stupidly".

Once you start to identify a behaviour as exactly that …

And not attribute it to your personality, you can start to be kinder to yourself. There is a truth that others can't love you until you love yourself. For Jane this was the beginning for her to see that she had control over not only what she thought of herself but what others thought of her too. And as I will show you further on in the book, how others perceive you has a huge impact on how well you communicate.

Another thing to consider is how your statements can become a self-fulfilling prophesy – if you say to yourself you can't do something often enough then you won't be able to do it. Now this isn't a book about how to feel better about yourself as such, there are lots of books out there on how to think and behave more positively. Some are more useful than others but if you tend to view yourself and your life negatively then I highly recommend you read The Luck Factor and Rip It Up, both by Richard Wiseman.[5] In the former he shows you four simple behavioural techniques that can help you to understand, control and increase your own good fortune and in the latter how to take positive action to make the changes that you want.

---

[5] The Luck Factor, Richard Wiseman. Published Random House. ISBN 978-0-09-944324-7 and Rip It Up, Richard Wiseman. Published Pan Macmillan. ISBN 978-1-4472-7336-3

What *this* book is, is a combination of tips and techniques that will help you to feel more comfortable communicating, whatever the situation. And learning to quell your inner voice is a key aspect of stopping yourself from undermining your own authority.

I also said at the start of this chapter that you need to feel comfortable being you and that isn't always as simple as it sounds.

To feel more comfortable being yourself I strongly recommend you consider using positive affirmations if you don't already. Up until now I have talked about how we subconsciously talk to ourselves and how what we say can become true even if it wasn't originally. Equally you can consciously talk to yourself and over time that can become the truth.

Over the years while running Partners With You we have worked with hundreds of people who want to improve at presenting and networking and we show them all how to use affirmations. Choose a positive affirmation that works for you and it could change your life.

A positive affirmation has some rules ...

It has to be positive, in the present and believable. Not "I will be more confident" but "I am confident". However, if your inner voice adds "Oh, no you're not!" then it's not believable so you'll need to change it to something else. Perhaps, "I am becoming more confident".

Try it now! Think of a statement about yourself that is positive, in the present and you believe to be true. It can be anything ... "I'm a good cook" or "I draw well" or "I am getting fitter" ... you get the picture.

Say it out loud and repeat it over and over again.

When you repeat a positive affirmation, you start to believe it more. You may notice that you start to smile, you change the emphasis, you use more vocal variety. So long as your inner voice isn't disagreeing with you then you will find you start to believe the statement.

For a while after leaving paid employment I sold my services as a consultant and interim manager "helping companies to stop annoying their customers" which meant that I was often helicoptered into a department that wasn't working well and given responsibility to get it fixed! I was working in a sector where I was pretty well known and a lot of the projects were for people I had worked for previously.

Great Aunt Gertie was having a field day … believe me I was doubting my every move. There was a large portion of inner voice chatter about how I wasn't up to the job and I used positive affirmations a lot!

I found walking from the station every morning to the client's office saying "I am coping brilliantly" to the beat of my steps (one step per syllable) made a huge difference to how I walked into the office and felt about myself. I wrote it in my diary and had it by my radio alarm clock at home so that I saw it as soon as I rolled over in the morning and it always put a smile on my face!

But remember it HAS to be believable to your inner voice or it just won't work.

Actions you can take from this chapter:

- Thank your inner voice for their concern but tell it you have things under control.
- Use the "seven-eleven" breathing technique.
- Don't say "I am xxx" try "That was xxx" or "I behaved in a xxx way".
- Read the Luck Factor and Rip It Up by Richard Wiseman.
- Use positive affirmations.

CHAPTER 3

The different ways we communicate.

Having settled into my corner office and begun to understand what others expected of me I soon realised that some of my colleagues didn't see the world as I did. One in particular kept telling me that I was negative. Now that's not how I see myself! A realist maybe but I always try to look at the positives in every situation … how could he have got me so wrong?

He though, from my perspective, was a poor judge of character and always assumed the best in others even when all signs pointed to them being someone you should cross the road to avoid. How could we both be in the same meeting and yet see such different things in what happened around us?

If only I had understood then …

How differently we all approach things and that I could affect the outcome of a discussion much more effectively than by just wishing the others would stop being so annoying!

I'll show you what I mean.

John walks into a room of colleagues and greets them. He asks them about their weekend and tells them about his. After a few minutes of "chit-chat" he starts the meeting. He always thinks it is odd that Mary never really adds much to this conversation and at best you get a "fine", in response to the question "How was your weekend?" His view of Mary is that she is good at her job but a bit of a cold fish … a problem at the moment when the project is delayed and you have to rely on your connections to get things moving again.

Mary on the other hand, thinks that John is too "touchy-feely". She could comfortably be 10 minutes late to any meeting that John is attending as there will be a lot of "waffle" about family and evenings out. She remembers once, John regaling them at a client meeting with a five-minute story about his child's bicycle accident and the subsequent visit to hospital. The child was fine so it was irrelevant to the task at hand, and the clients certainly didn't need to know about it.

Her view of John is that he wastes time and is far too chatty. Mary thinks she could name all of John's family although she has never met them … John has never learnt that if he chatted less and concentrated more on the agenda, they would have far fewer delays. As she is about to show them, the project is running even later than anticipated.

Robert finds Mary quite confrontational …

And wishes that she would be less monosyllabic, particularly with John. John doesn't give the impression that he minds but she is downright rude at times; she doesn't appear to make any effort. It is true that John is quite chatty and likes to be the centre of attention but he is pleasant with it, he just likes to get on with people … and you can't do that if you don't know them, can you? Robert just wishes she would make more effort and that John occasionally took enough breath to realise the world didn't revolve around him.

If only they were both a bit easier to work with, Mary comes across as aloof and John seems to relish embellishing his stories to annoy her. If they would both concentrate on the team and the client, anticipating the consequences of their decisions, then the project would be finished much more quickly.

Graham could happily knock everyone's heads together. If John isn't droning on about his witless child, then Mary is creating yet another Gant Chart or Robert is trying to placate them and worrying about the impact on some other part of the company that isn't important to the point in hand. Can't they just see that the reason the project is delayed is them and their inability to focus. If things carry on Graham can see that he is going to have step in and take charge.

Do you recognise yourself …

Or your colleagues in John, Mary, Graham and Robert? I can certainly think of a few people who are similar to each. And truthfully, I am more a mixture of Mary and Robert than I am John or Graham.

Is one approach better than another? Well it depends. None of them are "wrong" but if Mary reports to Robert, Graham or John, she may find her route to promotion is more difficult. If she is the boss then John may find himself side-lined. If Graham is the boss then the project may not be delayed but they will probably all feel an element of resentment towards him.

As a team, if they don't adapt their behaviour to the people they are working with, they will find the project is getting delayed because of the way they like to work and communicate, rather than their project management skills.

Chances are though …

That they just don't realise the impact that they have on those around them. They (like you and me) see the world from their own point of view and that's what I want to talk about in this chapter … because once you understand how you communicate and the impact that has, you are in a position to make decisions to create a different (and better) outcome.

You may think that you only communicate in one particular way. And each of us certainly has our preference. For example, I don't shout. Or at least not very often!! It doesn't really work for me. If I start shouting it's because I have lost control of my emotions and it rarely ends well for me (or anyone else). However, I have certainly worked for many people who felt very differently and weren't uncomfortable raising their voice.

Now don't get me wrong, I can shout, I just choose not to … most of the time.

Why is it that I choose not to and others move straight to bellowing in a single step?

I'm not going to discuss at length if we are a product of Nature or Nurture but there is no doubt that we are a combination of both our genes and our upbringing.

For example, how well you can physically hear is down to your genes. But how much you hear is likely to be down to your upbringing … I'll explain.

Imagine you live in an environment where you have little space …

And a desire to read. It is highly likely that you will learn to filter out the noise of those around you so that you can concentrate on a book. The phrase to "lose yourself in a book" to describe someone who is completely unaware of what is going on around them is well known for a reason. If you have learnt this skill then what you hear will be down to both your genes and your upbringing.

The way that you behave and communicate is dependent on what is going on in your head. And what you are thinking is dependent on what is going on around you and what your version of Great Aunt Gertie is telling you.

The Betari Box[6] is a classic model in conflict management and helps you to see what I am talking about. Imagine that you are in a bad mood and your head hurts. You turn to your colleague and ask him to quieten down as he's

---

[6] Also known as Betari's Box. The origin of the model is unknown.

giving you a headache but maybe you ask in a more aggressive tone of voice than you intended. He is surprised and hurt by your tone of voice and tells you so. Your head is hurting and you let your bad mood get the better of you and tell him not to be so pathetic. He reacts ... and the cycle continues. Unless one of you is willing to break the cycle a full blown, stand up row could be the consequence, or a complaint to HR about you or ... you get the picture.

Your upbringing, culture, religion, friends, school, books, magazines you read, TV shows you watched etc, etc, all affect your thought processes and view of the world. If you accept that, then it has to be a given that everyone views a situation from a slightly or greatly differing viewpoint. So, when someone else is telling you their truth it is only that ... their truth. And when you compare their truth to yours it can be diametrically opposed. Not because either of you is wrong but because you are seeing it from a different point of view.

Imagine you hear two people shouting at each other in the room next door. If you have only heard people raise their voice in anger you will probably say they are arguing. However, if you lived in a house where every mealtime you had to shout to be heard over the others at the table, then you probably won't hear an argument, just people who want to be heard.

So, everyone is different. We are affected by our different backgrounds, what is going on around us and our behaviour and communication style preferences.

You can't change who you are so what can you do?

Well the rest of this book will help and I highly recommend going to the Partners With You website [www.partnerswithyou.co.uk/prism-brain-mapping/quiz] to get a **free** overview of your communication style. Are you more like Robert, John, Graham or Mary ... or a combination?

I have used *PRISM* Brain Mapping for the past 10 years to help me explain to my clients how they choose to behave and communicate and how to adapt their choices to get a different outcome.

Once you understand how you choose to communicate then you can start adapting your approach accordingly.

For starters, when someone reacts in a way you are surprised or upset by or they just handle a conversation differently to the way you would, remember that it is just their preference.

We'll talk in Chapter 5 about how to adapt your behaviour for different communication styles but just being aware and willing to change will have a beneficial effect on your communications.

And of course, if someone is very difficult you can always gift your copy of this book or recommend they complete the free *PRISM* Brain Mapping quiz!

— 30 —

Actions you can take from this chapter:

- Accept that you approach each situation from your point of view. Others may not see it in the same way.
- Consider how your background and upbringing might affect the way that you choose to communicate and behave in different situations.
- Go to www.partnerswithyou.co.uk/prism-brain-mapping/quiz and complete the questionnaire to receive your personal communication style report.

Your report from the free quiz will be very illuminating. If your interest is piqued and you want to know more, get in touch. You can then complete a 20-30 minutes online quiz to receive a full report detailing your underlying and adapted behaviour at work and a great deal more information about your choices of behaviour styles.

CHAPTER 4

First impressions.

Let me tell you about Jacob.

He is slightly dishevelled.

Not dirty … it's just that his navy suit and pale blue shirt are crumpled and his striped tie is crooked. His hair touches the top of his collar at the back and curls just over the top of his ears, he is clean shaven with just the beginnings of a late afternoon stubble.

His brown shoes are worn and shabby, although clean.

I am watching him from across the bar as he chats to two other men. He is sitting quite upright on the stool with his lower arm resting on the high table top. They are laughing and sipping their drinks. He's not wearing any jewellery, not even a watch. They are too far away for me to be able to hear what they are saying but they appear to be comfortable in each other's company and none of them seem keen to leave.

Now let me ask you some questions …

- How old do you think Jacob is?
- Do you think Jacob is single?
- Which do you think he is more likely to be – a teacher, a salesman or a banker?
- Does he live alone or with others? – His Mother, his partner or dog?
- Is he living on the bread line, earning 'enough' or loaded?

There is no right or wrong answer to these questions … I don't know either. Jacob is a made-up name for a man I saw across a bar when I was waiting for friends.

But unless you answered "I don't know" to all those questions (which I don't think you did) you were making assumptions about him based on just my description.

Everyone makes decisions about others without them having to open their mouth. If you don't believe me then imagine you have walked into a room full of people you don't know (a meeting or event). There are only chairs free next to other people … who do you choose to sit next to?

How did you decide who you felt most comfortable to approach?

You will have looked at them and decided who is most like you (or who is least like you) and to do that you will have made unconscious decisions about who they are, what they do, what their job is and a whole lot more. It is just what we do!

According to Amy Cuddy in her book Presence[7] we are assessing each other for warmth and competence. Or how trustworthy you appear and whether (in a work scenario) you are any good at your job.

There is lots of research available …

And it all points to the fact that as soon as you are in view, others are assessing you and making assumptions. You slope into the room quietly looking at the floor … and they will think you are in the wrong place. You walk in banging the door against the wall and they will worry that they are in the wrong place!

So, it stands to reason that your first impression will have a huge impact on the relationship you have with others. You can change the impression but it takes a much longer time. I liken it to a dial; it's as though the person you are meeting has a dial that goes down to -10 and up to +10 and when you walk into view you are at zero.

---

[7] Presence by Amy Cuddy. Publisher: Orion Publishing Co. ISBN: 9781409156000

If you look a mess, are running because you are late and …

Arrive in reception frazzled and puffing … the dial may move down to -3. If you then babble on about the journey and how difficult it was to get here due to family issues the dial will go down again to maybe, -6. It's going to be hard to get to +10 no matter how good you are after that.

Whereas if you walk in looking composed, dressed for the role and arrive in reception with a smile, the dial may already be moved up to +4 before you even open your mouth. Now you don't have to work so hard to stay on the plus side of the dial.

So, how do you ensure that you make a great first impression … and then what do you do to build up a great relationship?

Well let's take them one at a time …

You want to look confident when you meet someone, stand up to present or walk in a room. You want to look as though you belong but equally you don't want to look as though you think you own the place or be thought of as arrogant. An excellent starting point is to take a positive standing position (and then return there every now and again).

For a positive standing position, you need 3 images in your mind:

1. **3 points on the bottom of your feet, like a tripod** – on the big toe, little toe and middle of the heel. You want to have your feet below your hips and shoulders and stand on all 3 points on both feet. This stops your feet wandering and wobbling and also ensures that you are firmly grounded as you stand.

Have a look in the mirror to check where your feet are normally … generally women stand with their feet too close together as though apologising for the space taken and men stand with them wider … this makes you look more confident but there is only a fine line between looking confident and arrogant.

2. **Now imagine there is a string running from the floor** up between your legs, through your body and out at the top of your head. Someone taller than you is pulling it up. Make sure the string is coming out from the centre of your head and not the front as that will raise your nose and make you look snooty. Not the look for a positive standing position!

3. **Finally imagine you are wearing a bolero jacket** (a short jacket like a Matador might wear for a bull fight) and someone comes from behind and pulls it softly at the bottom, in the centre. Just so the shoulders are pulled back gently, opening up your chest and lungs.

The joy of this position is that you look confident and capable but it is difficult to make a negative assumption about who you are or how trustworthy you might be.

Go back to the mirror …

Stand as you would normally and then stand in this positive standing position. It's not about pretending to be someone you aren't, but about being the best version of you … particularly when you meet them for the first time.

Once you start chatting to someone or get into your presentation you will move around and your posture will change; but this is a great position both to start from and then return to at various points. When I am out networking,

I will often catch myself standing in a less positive position and remember to pull my string and bolero, so that I look more approachable.

If you are sitting the same rules apply.

Both feet on the floor and your bolero jacket on. Put your bottom as far back as you can in the chair while making sure your feet are still on the floor and this time the string runs from under your seat, through your body and out from the top of your head. Leaving your hands resting on your lap will give you a positive sitting position and again nothing negative can be read from it.

There are other things you can do to make a great impression.

Unless you are working in very different cultures, it is pretty safe to say that in Northern Europe and America you are expected to look people in the eye when you speak, smile as you greet someone and shake hands firmly.

Eye contact is all important. If you are speaking you will look away to retrieve the information from your memory but constantly looking away and not looking the listener in the eye will affect their perception of you. In an office in the UK, if you don't look someone in the eye, the chances are they will think you look "shifty" and are hiding something.

In the workshops delivered by Partners With You we run an exercise where you speak to a partner with constant eye contact and then again but with no eye contact at all.

The feedback we get is always the same …

1. It's hard to think of the right words when you are staring at someone (because you can't look away to retrieve any information)

2. It's uncomfortable as the listener, to be stared at constantly … particularly if you don't know the person speaking and
3. With no eye contact it is much harder to hear what is being said.

This is particularly important if you are delivering a presentation. It's really easy to start a presentation, notice someone is smiling and nodding as you speak and because that is comforting, start to look mainly at them. And in doing that, you stop looking at the rest of the audience. Apart from the obvious discomfort the person you are looking at will feel as you speak just to them, the rest of the audience will start to switch off because with no eye contact you can't hear well.

As well as eye contact a real smile is important … particularly if you are meeting someone.

But don't fake it!

A fake smile means you look more like an animal about to attack than someone who wants to build a new relationship.

In my experience, the only way to have a real smile is to actually think of something that makes you happy! The good news is that no-one knows what you are thinking so it can be anything. As you enter a room or meet someone for the first time, think of something that really makes you happy and your smile will reach your eyes. And that will put your dial position up rather than down.

Finally, before I leave the subject of first impressions, a quick word about handshakes …

Make sure yours is firm and confident.

You would be amazed how many people equate your handshake to your ability to do your job or deliver your service (even if it's not you that will ultimately deliver the service)!

A wet fish is not only off putting but it indicates that you aren't trustworthy or very capable. Meanwhile a grip that is too firm will hurt anyone wearing jewellery and could appear that you are aggressive or trying to overcompensate.

Practice on a friend or a member of your family and ask them how you come across. It is one of those things that you are assumed to be able to do; and in my experience that isn't always true!

Of course, there are other things to consider when communicating to help you build rapport and you may not always get it right but the fact you are trying will have a big impact.

Listening skills, which I cover later, should be a given (there is no point asking lots of questions if you don't listen well) but for the time being concentrate on making a great first impression and keeping the dial above "0".

Actions you can take from this chapter:

- Accept that you make assumptions and so does everyone else.
- Do what you can to ensure that the assumptions others make about you are fair and positive.
- Concentrate on the actual person you are speaking to and not the person you assume they are from your first impression.
- Use the Tripod, String and Bolero at the start of a conversation, presentation or to return to when you notice you aren't looking as positive as you could.
- Practice greeting people with great eye contact, smile and handshake.
- If you aren't sure about how to make a great first impression then sign up to the www.stepoutfromtheshadows.co.uk where there are 6 videos showing you exactly how to make a great first impression.

CHAPTER 5

Building relationships and adapting your behaviour

So, let's assume that you have made a great first impression and you now want to start building rapport. According to the Cambridge English

Dictionary the definition of rapport is *"a good understanding of someone and an ability to communicate well with them"*, which I take to mean two things.

When you are meeting someone new …

That you need to ask lots of open questions to get them to talk about themselves and then adapt how you communicate to suit them.

And when you are better acquainted …

I interpret that to mean you should take the time to try to understand how the other person likes to communicate and then adapt what you do and say to get a better outcome.

Let's take each separately …

When meeting someone new.

Remember John from the start of chapter 3? He liked to chat … so if you met him and asked him how he was, he is likely to answer you with more than "fine" or "OK", whereas Mary is definitely likely to answer the question with just one word or one word and then thanks! These are great indicators of how they like to communicate.

Imagine that you are at a conference and you have started chatting to the person you are standing next to in the queue for coffee. If you are talking to a 'John' it will be fairly easy to move from what he thought of the key note speaker. He is going to want to share a level of personal information with you early on in your relationship and if you ask him questions about this and perhaps drop in a little more about you the person, then you will find it easier to build rapport (or communicate well with him).

On the other hand, if you are standing next to a 'Mary' she is going to want to know you a LOT better before sharing any personal information with you. If this is the case then you steer the conversation onto her work, what she sees as the benefits of implementing the ideas from the speaker and such like; keeping it business focussed and relevant.

When building rapport with people I don't know, the best advice …

I ever received was to imagine that you are holding a spotlight and your job is to shine it on the other person for as long as you can. This means that you let them choose the topics of conversation, you ask them questions that elicit more than a simple yes/no answer and don't get onto personal subjects unless they steer the conversation that way.

I often quote from Rudyard Kipling's poem 'I Keep Six Honest Serving Men'[8] when talking about how to keep that spotlight on the other person.

> *I keep six honest serving–men*
> *(They taught me all I knew);*
> *Their names are What and Why and When*
> *And How and Where and Who.*

If you ask questions that start with any one of these "serving-men" then you open up the opportunity to build a conversation; that's why they are known as Open Questions. For example, if you ask "Did you enjoy the workshop?" you are likely to get a yes or no answer. On the other hand, if you ask "What

---

[8] www.kiplingsociety.co.uk/poems_serving.htm

did you find most interesting during the workshop?" you are much more likely to get an insight into the other person rather than a one-word answer.

One caveat to add here is not to use "Why" questions too often as they can quickly make you sound (and feel) like an interrogator!

Another tip when meeting people is to be adaptable ...

Don't try to push the conversation in the direction you want it to go. Which, at times, is easier said than done. If you are talking to someone who works in a company that you would like to work with then your agenda may be very different to theirs. You may want to move the conversation around so that you can tell them all about you or your company's skill set but every time you try to force this topic your companion starts talking about something else.

Imagine you were telling a story ...

But rather than starting and finishing it, you had to take turns with someone else to tell it one sentence at a time. The end result of the story would be very different to the story you thought you were going to tell at the start and you might be tempted to try to pull the story line back at times.

If you do that during a conversation then it will begin to feel forced and all about you (which is absolutely not what happens when you shine the light on the other person). You have to just go where the conversation takes you and accept that this small talk will ultimately help you to build trust and as Amy Cuddy says, first and foremost, we are assessing each other for warmth.

You want the conversation to flow well ...

And if you are listening well and asking lots of open questions without trying to force the direction, then the result will be the other person will start to open up so that you can gain a good understanding of them. That in turn will help you to communicate well and you've started to create rapport between you.

In contrast, if you keep trying to pitch yourself, your idea or proposition the chances are that the other person will quickly make their excuses and move away.

What about when you already know them.

If you are trying to build rapport with people you work with, then think about how they are going to want to be communicated with. If you were working with John, Mary, Robert and Graham from the last chapter and needed to get them on board you would do it differently.

The table below shows you what I mean and of course if you have taken the free quiz on the Partners With You site[9], you will already have some idea of how you like to communicate. Knowing that will help you know when you need to do the most adapting and when you don't.

---

[9] www.partnerswithyou.co.uk/prism-brain-mapping/quiz

Who	How they like to communicate	How to adapt for them
John	is chatty, shares information about himself and his family, doesn't move straight into the point in hand, likes to tell you about his weekend. He isn't detail orientated; he might be optimistic about hitting deadlines but probably has a gut feeling rather than any specific evidence.	Allow time for social chit-chat and keep the atmosphere positive. John will probably have some great ideas and contacts so make sure that he feels included.
Mary	doesn't give a lot away, unless she knows you very well you probably know very little about her life away from work. She is detail orientated and doesn't like to go with her gut. She needs to look at the information before she makes a decision. If she says she is optimistic about hitting target then she has good reason and can explain these to you!	Give Mary time to go through any information before you meet and walk her logically through the plan, don't flit from topic to topic. Mary won't like emotional displays so concentrate on the business case with pros and cons for any suggestions or ideas.
Robert	is a collaborator and likes to get things done through consultation and cooperation. He too will comfortably share personal information but will ask questions about you too. A definite people person, he will want to make a decision having spoken to his team so not one for an off the cuff decision.	Get to the point quickly and as with Mary, give Robert time to think about his response. Let him speak, be patient and non-argumentative.
Graham	wants to get things done. He is focussed on getting from A – B and understands that some people may not be happy with his route but they will come around to it when they understand what the alternative is. Doesn't understand why people take so long to make decisions and take everything so personally.	Don't expect Graham to wade through the information – management summaries were designed for people like him. But be prepared to support your case. Be quick, be specific and be brief!

Table 1[10]

---

[10] Adapted from original source provided by *PRISM* Brain Mapping

Try it yourself …

Think about having to present a report for four different people you know who fit the following criteria:

A. Accurate, careful and orderly. They like to consider all the information, analyse it and talk through the precise details not the general ideas.
B. Impatient, abrupt and quick tempered. They like to take charge and drive towards a goal.
C. An ideas person. They are outgoing, creative, enthusiastic and fun-loving.
D. Someone who is consultative and likes to talk things through with the team. They are kind-hearted, patient, helpful and accommodating.

Have you thought of colleagues that fit the four descriptions?

How might you present the report?

If you want them to act on the information you are providing, you'll want to provide it differently for each of them.

If I was presenting the report, I would make sure that I had covered all bases:

For example, I would make sure that I had all the background data available but, in the knowledge, that those most like A and D would want the time to go through it before we met, so I would provide the report for them in advance.

I would have a management summary for the B's I was presenting to with just a few bullet points focusing on the objectives, actions and solutions. I know that they will never wade through the background data or a lengthy report but will expect me to be able to support the conclusions drawn.

And finally, for the C in the room I would start the presentation, painting the picture of my suggestions and aim to keep everything as upbeat and positive as possible.

If you make the effort to adapt the way you deliver the information for the many "types" of people then you will find that difficult conversations are minimised. If you are a manager this will reduce the "people problems" that you encounter and if you are managing up the system your ideas will be more quickly accepted and you will probably find you have more advocates across the company.

Actions you can take from this chapter:

- Have some open questions up your sleeve that you can ask people in order to start a conversation.
- Adapt your approach according to how the other person reacts to you and don't try to force the conversation onto topics of your choice.
- When building rapport with your colleagues consider how they will want to receive your input.
- Consider everyone as you build your presentation so that you can get everyone on board.

CHAPTER 6

Assertiveness skills

Say what you mean and mean what you say!

Hmmm … easier said than done, I hear you say.

Whatever type of communication style you prefer, there are times when being assertive isn't easy.

Years ago, I was sent on an Assertiveness workshop and our Sales Manager told me that I was already bossy enough!

Now, don't get me started on the implications of this comment in terms of blatant sexism (no man ever gets called bossy) or the implication that an assertive woman is a bossy woman. However, it's an indication of a problem some colleagues have regarding you as being assertive or displaying assertive behaviour, and why some people avoid trying to be assertive … they misunderstand what it is.

Assertive behaviour is the ability to state your case, opinion or point of view in a way that means that you are heard and crucially, you are still in a position to hear the other point of view as well.

You can't be assertive when you are emotional.

If you wait until your emotions kick in then you will either turn the emotion onto others (and speak out in anger) or turn it into yourself and go over and over the conversation in your head with lots of ways you could have handled it better (and your Great Aunt Gertie will have a field day too!)

It has nothing to do with being aggressive or dictatorial or forcing your point of view on others. Of course, there may be a good time for that … if I'm stuck in a burning tower, I don't want the fire fighter to discuss my opinion on the pros and cons of the routes out … I want them to tell me which way to run … clearly and loudly!

But most of the time at work we aren't in a burning building and being shouted at isn't going to work long term.

Having said that, many of the issues I have come across have been caused by a lack of assertive behaviour … by the inability to take someone aside and have a quiet word to address a problem before it became an issue.

Everyone can be assertive, just not all of the time.

Sometimes it is the situation that stops you or the person you're talking to, or who that person reminds you of. If you are talking to someone who reminds you of your headmaster at school then it might be very easy to feel like your teenage self and hard to behave assertively with them.

I know for a number of my clients being assertive is difficult because it might cause an argument and they don't like conflict. They avoid speaking their mind because the other person might disagree. The result is they get annoyed with themselves (which isn't helpful) and the problem doesn't disappear … it just gets bigger.

If you are a manager this is even more of a concern.

An example I use resonates for many people.

Imagine you have a member of staff (Pat) who is late every morning. Not by much but always 5 or 10 minutes late. You don't want to cause a fuss so you don't mention it. (Or worse you say something like "Nice of you to turn up!" or "Good Afternoon!" in response to their cheery good morning).

Whatever your response you don't formally address the fact that they are late and your team notice.

They may not say anything but they will definitely notice.

A few weeks later another team member (Sammy) is late back from lunch by 20 minutes and you ask them if they are OK. They aren't and they lash out at you, angry that you have mentioned that they are 20 minutes late when you have ignored the fact that Pat is always late!

Note you didn't mention that they were late, you just asked if Sammy was OK but that's not what Sammy heard.

Now you are hurt, Sammy is hurt and Pat is feeling bad.

No one wins and they are all still being late. Pretty soon drifting start times mean that people turn up late to work, back from lunch and to meetings.

In that situation, the assertive thing to do in the first place would have been to take Pat aside and ask if there was a problem getting in on time when she started arriving late. There may be a simple explanation like the bus only runs hourly, she can't get the earlier one due to family commitments and the next one arrives at 9:00 which means she walks in a little late. If that's the case, you might be able to change her start time, lunch break and/or end time so she isn't late but on time at 9:15. And you can then let the team know what's happening.

But if you don't ask you won't know and the problem won't get addressed.

You don't have to be heavy handed – the assertive approach is not that at all. Instead it's the ability to find a solution that works for both you and Pat. If you can approach every conversation open to finding a solution that works for you both, it will make your life easier and less stressful.

If you are Pat in this situation then the assertive thing to do is to ask to meet with your manager and explain the situation with the bus and ask if you can start 10 minutes later and have a shorter lunch break, or something that will work for both you and the company. All too often you hope a problem isn't noticed, whilst it actually is, but no one mentions it until it's too big to ignore.

So being open to finding a solution for all is a great starting point for being more assertive. But what else can you do?

The first and most important thing is when you are making a request. Conflict and arguments arise because the person asked doesn't understand either the urgency or the constraints that you are under.

Let me give you an example.

You are preparing for a really important sales meeting and one of your colleagues has offered to help you get ready for it. You spoke to them this morning and asked them to source and load the graphics. They said "Of course". Now it's 3pm and you have just walked over to get the final set.

Except they haven't started yet.

This is a real situation that happened to a client of mine and she was still livid when we talked about it weeks later. And these feelings and situations damage working relationships.

The problem was that her colleague hadn't understood the urgency. He knew she had said she needed them by end of play but without understanding what was happening next, he had thought the following morning would be just as good and planned to get it done by 9:30 tomorrow. He wasn't aware that the handouts were being sent out that evening to the printers so the graphics had to be uploaded by the end of today.

My client had forgotten to give her colleague her why.

She had told them what she wanted and when … but not why it was needed by then!

So, her colleague hadn't understood the urgency and had made an assumption on what he knew. Had she said she needed them by end of play today because everything was being sent out tonight to the printers … he would have understood the why and raised it up his list of priorities.

So always ask for what you want, when you want it and WHY!

The second thing to remember is that when you are asking a favour you may want to couch the request with preamble, but most people on the receiving end don't appreciate the waffle.

You know the sort of thing I mean…

> *Do you think you … could you possibly manage, but only*
> *if you have time, I don't want to put too much work on*
> *your plate but it is urgent? But if it's not too much trouble*
> *could you get the report done by end of play today … or*
> *tomorrow if it's too much, or do you want to let me know*
> *if you think you can fit it in later?*

It is so irritating being on the receiving end of this. When do you want it by, today or tomorrow? Is it urgent or not? Do you need me to do it or not?

Most people just want to know what you want so they can help you if they can. If you beat about the bush and waffle when you ask then those who get annoyed by such unassertive behaviour are going to walk all over you and the rest will ignore you.

A simple …

> *Are you able to get the report done by end of play today*
> *as Jay wants a final read through before it is sent over for*
> *the 10am deadline?*

… is all that's needed so the other person is able to give you their honest answer regarding what they can or can't do by your deadline.

Which brings me to the third thing to remember … and that is to say NO when you mean NO!

Most people don't like to say No.

If they can help you, they will; but it is easy to feel you have to say Yes if it's your boss or someone you care about. Or if you feel it will affect your position in the company, you can feel you have to say Yes too.

In fact, some companies I know have a rule where you never say No. The idea behind this is to build a culture where everyone is looking for a solution, all possibilities are looked at and a positive energy is developed so the company can grow bigger and move faster, making the working environment somewhere you all want to be.

The trouble with this approach is you can end up with staff who believe that they HAVE to say Yes to every request which is neither healthy for the staff nor the company!

If you don't believe you are able to say No then two things will happen:

1. You will become overwhelmed.
2. You will let someone down, because you said you could do something and you couldn't … or if you did, it was sub-standard and you both know it.

I'm not suggesting that the next time you are asked to do something for your boss that you refuse point blank and just say NO!

What I suggest is that you consider whether you can; ask some questions about when it is needed by, what is actually required and where it sits in terms of priority alongside your other projects. Only then can you make a decision.

If you don't think you can do it then say so!

If you can offer a solution then do that too …

> *No, I'm sorry I can't do that today but if it can wait until tomorrow, I can do it for you then.*

OR

> *I'm already busy with xxx. Which is more important to you as I can definitely finish one of them today.*

You may find it difficult to say No but it is much worse to say Yes and then not deliver. If you say No, it means that I have a chance to find another solution, ask someone else, do it myself or speak to my boss about the fact it can't be done. If you say Yes, I leave believing it will be done … and that can lead to a whole mess of trouble if it's not.

Remember if your internal voice is stopping you from saying No then go back to Chapter 2 and see if you can work on quietening it down.

And if assertive behaviour is an area you know you need to work on then I would highly recommend you read Assertiveness at work: A Practical Guide To Handling Awkward Situations by Ken Back and Kate Back[11].

---

[11] Assertiveness at Work by Ken Back and Kate Back McGraw-Hill, 2005. ISBN: 9780077114280

Actions you can take from this chapter:

- Raise any issues or concerns before you get emotional.
- Be open to finding a solution that works for everyone (it may well look very different to what you first had in mind).
- When you make a request always give your Why!
- Don't waffle when asking for something. Be concise.
- Don't say Yes when you mean No.
- Go back to Chapter 2 if you can't quieten your inner voice
- Read Assertiveness at Work by Ken Back & Kate Back.

CHAPTER 7

Being seen and heard

Are you often the last to volunteer, hate walking into a room full of strangers and/or find the idea of selling too hateful to consider?

Then this chapter is for you!

I'm talking about the fear of speaking up, saying what you think … in particular in meetings whether that's a formal meeting or in passing at the water cooler.

I spend a lot of my time working with people who understand that they are their own sales person. Lots of them are small business owners; mainly selling a service or their own expertise. They need to take every opportunity to connect so that they can build networks and relationships. Pretty easy to see that they are selling.

But I also work with graduates looking for work, people looking to change career or who just want to be taken more seriously. All of these people are salespeople too … but they are selling themselves, their ideas and their potential.

In fact, you are selling even if you aren't looking for a change or a new role. As a mother and wife, I have to sell often. If you have ever tried to negotiate with a teenager you know you are a salesperson!

To sell your ideas, service or expertise then you need to be willing to "Step Out from The Shadows" and put your head above the parapet … just saying what you want or voicing your point of view takes guts. It's imperative for every business that its staff are able to speak up and speak out. Being surrounded by 'Yes' men or women makes for an easy life initially, but the reality is you need to know when problems arise.

So how can you be seen and heard more easily?

Firstly, think about how you want to be perceived.

I've talked about how to make a great first impression with your posture, eye contact and smile, but what about the way you are dressed? I'm not a stylist but I have worked with Helen Reynolds of Helen Reynolds Style[12] and I know what colours and styles suit me. There are lots of colour consultants and stylists out there who can help. And if you really want to feel good about the way you look, understanding what works and doesn't can save you both time and money.

Having said that you don't need to be 'suited and booted' at all times. Whether you are male or female, the key thing is understanding what clothes and colours suit you, so that whatever you wear you will look and feel good in.

To be well dressed is to be appropriately dressed.

If you are a plumber the appropriate clothes to wear may well be a boiler suit; but a black one may make you look ill while in navy you look amazing.

You want to consider who the others in the room are going to be … if in doubt my advice is, it is better to be overdressed than underdressed. It is easier to look confident as the only one in the room in a suit, than the only one in jeans and a t-shirt.

Remember you can wear whatever you want but that others will be using your style and clothing to build their assumptions about you; just as you did at the start of Chapter 4 when I described Jacob.

So, let's assume you are dressed appropriately and you have walked into the room (be it a meeting room or the staff kitchen). The way you walk in matters. If you sidle in and avoid all eye contact you will look as though you are apologising for your existence and it is hard to sell yourself if the others in the room don't think you rate yourself. After all, if you don't why would they?

[12] https://helenreynoldsstyle.com/

Remember to pull your Bolero and look ahead.

If you look as though you should be in the room others will assume your legitimacy. Another great tip I heard from a professor who worked in a very male environment is to speak as soon as you can when you arrive in the room.

It can be as simple as asking to borrow a pen or if anyone minds if you close the window. It doesn't matter so long as you can be heard. She didn't know why it worked but she always felt that the others in the room had become acclimatised to her voice and therefore heard her better. I've tried it and it works!

While on the topic of voice, another tip I learnt from the team of actors I work with is to hum at a low register before I walk into a room; particularly if I am expecting a heated discussion. When women get cross, angry, nervous or excited they get shriller. And in my experience the shriller I become the less others listen to me.

I wish I had known this when I was one of only two women on a management team of ten. Each week we would meet to discuss future projects and without fail a heated debate would start over the staffing needs to deliver the new opportunities. And as the conversations got more heated, I would get crosser still when someone told me to "calm down" or "not to get my knickers in a twist" or some other similarly charming comment!

What I didn't realise is that the angrier I got …

The higher my voice got and the more I sounded, to my colleagues, like their wives, mothers or daughters … and the more they switched off. Had I known; I could have hummed at a lower register before the meeting. That would have meant I started the meeting at a lower register and it would have taken longer to get to the point when my colleagues stopped listening!

Another mistake you can make ...

When you want to get your point across is to use pre-qualifiers. Women tend to use them more than men but anyone who isn't sure of the reaction they will get can find themselves inserting them. And the problem with pre-qualifiers is that they diminish your authority. Particularly if you are talking to someone who is similar to Graham (say it quickly, clearly and once) from Chapter 3.

When I talk about pre-qualifiers, I mean saying things like:

"I just wanted to say ..." or
"I don't know if you agree but ..." or
"This may sound stupid but ..." or
"Just off the top of my head maybe we could ..." or
"I don't know if someone has already said this but ..."

Invariably, you are saying these things to tone down what you are about to say, as a buffer before you say something controversial or you're worried about being assertive. Or you might be saying them to quieten your Great Aunt Gertie who tends to pipe up just before you say anything.

It undermines your credibility and authority.

Imagine you are in a meeting and everyone has been asked to suggest a solution to the new process. Which sounds more credible ...?

> *"I'm not sure I'm right but I would have thought that by checking the xxx at the start we could remove the bottleneck later."*

OR

> *"By checking the xxx at the start we could remove the bottleneck later."*

The authority you will have by removing pre-qualifiers from your speech patterns will surprise you. If you use them habitually it will take some effort and you won't manage it every time but watch out for it and remove them whenever you can.

Another way to lose credibility is to become too emotional.

I have discussed at length with my girlfriends and clients why many angry women cry. It's not that we are upset … it's that we are angry, and woe betide anyone who tries to calm us down!

In October 2019, Marissa Korbel wrote in her article for Guernica[13] "Why we cry when we are angry" …

> *"While over 51 percent of women have experienced angry tears, under two percent of men have. Even as crying has become more socially acceptable for men, it is only acceptable in response to sadness or pain. When angry, men are much more likely to act out physically in aggressive ways. Women are more likely to cry."*

---

[13] www.guernicamag.com/why-we-cry-when-were-angry

And it doesn't matter if you are crying or punching, your authority will be diminished and your ability to speak up next time will reduce too. So, what can you do?

If you have read the book to this point you will know some of the techniques already covered will help you at the moment you start to get emotional.

But there is one technique I have used and found to be really effective that has stopped me getting to the point where I'm too angry to speak.

Repetition is really helpful ...

And works really well in those moments when you aren't being listened to ... but only so long as you haven't got too emotional. Repeat what you want or need, calmly and without anger.

I've used it on a number of occasions myself, one time that stands out was on the telephone with British Gas. They had been to fix my boiler; left having said it was fixed and within 20 minutes it had broken again. At the time I had two young children and it was expected to be -8 degrees that evening. We had been without heating and hot water for several days and I wanted it fixed.

Eventually I got through to customer service and asked for the engineer to return and was told he couldn't until the next day. To every response I calmly said that I understood what they were saying but repeated my request ... "I understand it's difficult but I need the engineer to return today". They used every excuse and I kept coming back with "…. I need the engineer to return today." And eventually (and I do mean eventually) the engineer agreed to return.

Result! It works in the office too. But you must stay calm and keep control of your vocal tone, otherwise it can easily escalate into an argument. And then you lose all your hard-won authority and credibility.

It's an approach that needs practice but I promise, you will reap benefits at home and at work as you master it.

Actions you can take from this chapter:

- Think about how you want to be perceived and consider getting some style advice.
- Walk into a room with your head held high and look people in the eye
- Consider humming low before a difficult meeting where you may raise your voice.
- Avoid using pre-qualifiers.
- Repeat what you want calmly and confidently. Let them know you have heard and understand what they have said … and then repeat what you want.

CHAPTER 8

Key Communication skills

Do you know the nursery rhyme 'For want of the nail, the shoe was lost'?

> For want of a nail, the shoe was lost;
> For want of the shoe, the horse was lost;
> For want of the horse, the rider was lost;
> For want of the rider, the battle was lost;

> For want of the battle, the kingdom was lost;
> And all for the want of a horseshoe nail[14].

References to the rhyme go back to the 1400's so we have known for a long time the importance of the little things. And this was never truer than when talking about communication.

When texting or emailing, for want of vocal tone the meaning is lost. When on the telephone, for want of facial expression the context is lost and when on a webinar or video call, for want of a clear background the focus is lost.

So, this chapter is about all the ways you communicate when …

You aren't in the same room as the other person or people. When you are on the telephone, using FaceTime or video, webinars, text or email.

I've divided it into 4 areas – listening skills, on-line or video, telephone and email or text. Many of the things I'm going to mention are relevant when face to face but made worse because of the lack of connection possible according to the tools used. The list isn't exhaustive but if you get your communication right when you are emailing or phoning people you will find it much easier to communicate when you meet them face to face.

Listening skills

Of course, this is important when face to face but it is even more essential when talking over the phone because the other person doesn't get any of the visual cues that you are listening to them.

---

14 www.wordsforlife.org.uk/songs/want-nail-shoe-was-lost

I know from the exercises we run in our workshops that people don't hear as well when they have no eye contact. This is why eye contact when you are speaking is so important and why it is so easy to stop listening when you don't have any.

I give you some techniques for listening when on the phone later in this chapter but for the time being let's focus on your active listening skills wherever you are.

Make sure you are in the right frame of mind to listen. If you are in the middle of something then ask the other person if you can get back to them at a more convenient time.

If they call, walk into your office or up to your desk, don't carry on typing (or filing or whatever you are doing) while they speak. You won't hear them properly. At best you will miss elements of what they have said, at worst you will end up agreeing to do something you can't or they will leave unsatisfied with the encounter.

If you are doing the interrupting (in person or on the phone) ALWAYS ask if it's convenient. Allow them to opt out of the conversation right now and arrange a more convenient time to call or speak in person.

Once you have agreed that now is convenient ...

Then commit to the conversation. Stop what you are doing and concentrate on what is being said. Watch for any body language you can see, listen for changes in vocal tone, hesitation and the like.

Even if they can't see you, you can show you are concentrating by asking questions and clarifying your understanding. You can reflect back what they are saying to make sure that you have understood them. Use phrases like … "So, what you are saying is …" or "Let me check that I have understood". You don't want to repeat what they have said word for word but you do want to use their word choices and phrases when you paraphrase so that they know that you have really heard them.

For example, if they say "I was really excited to be given the project but I am feeling very overwhelmed" when you paraphrase you don't want to change "excited" to "thrilled" or "overwhelmed" to "too busy". They won't feel as listened to and your choice of words may not mean the same thing to them.

By asking questions, clarifying and reflecting back what is being said to you, you are also less likely to be formulating your thoughts and jumping in with your response. Be patient and let the other person finish speaking before you respond. This way they will feel truly heard.

I like to use this acronym to help me remember what a LUCID conversation should be:

Listen to **U**nderstand, **C**larify and **I**nterpret and only then **D**iscuss.

On-line or video

I once ran a webinar with a speaker who had bags hanging on the door of her shared office and although we could only see her slides, every time someone walked in (which happened quite often) you could hear the bags clanking against each other. It was really distracting!

Video calls are becoming much more common and there are 3 key things to think about.

1. Can they see me?
2. What else can they see?
3. Where are my hands?

1. **Can they see me?**

What is the lighting like in your office, living room or the venue you are calling from? As I've said before, it is really important that whoever you are speaking to can see your eyes or they won't hear you and that's just as true when you are on a screen. But it's harder through the screen … if you want to look someone in the eye you need to look directly at the camera lens and not your phone or computer screen.

If you have glasses that transition into sunglasses be wary of facing a window when it is sunny, as the glasses will slowly start to hide your eyes. And remember if you are sitting in front of a window you will be a silhouette to them which means they won't be able to see any of your features!

2. **What else can they see?**

Think about what's behind you. Do you look like you are in an office or your bedroom? I can't tell you how often I have been looking at a dressing gown, bed, or even (once) a pile of dirty laundry behind the person I am speaking to. Have a quick look at what is behind you before you start your call.

Let others in the house or office know you are on a call. It is really distracting to watch someone walk into the room, realise they are now part of the background and with a look of horror walk backwards. It means I'm so busy watching what is going on behind you that I miss what you are saying!

And one to watch out for when you are in a café is who can see your screen. Recently I was on a call with a colleague in a café and the only seat she could find had a window behind her. Unfortunately, a gentleman in the street found her screen fascinating and that distracted everyone else on the call … and had we been looking at a document we could have crossed all sorts of privacy barriers.

If you do a lot of video calls then consider using something like Zoom[15] for your calls as you can create a virtual background with any royalty free picture and a piece of dark cloth or wall.

3. **Where are my hands?**

Your hands are your trust indicators so don't hide them from view and do use them to aid your speech. If you gesticulate in normal conversation then do so on a video call. Try to set the webcam or phone so your upper body and hands can be seen.

These three areas are particularly important if you have a call with a new prospect, employer or you expect it to be a difficult conversation. If you aren't used to speaking online then get a friend to help you practise a couple of times and give you feedback on how you come across.

Telephone

Telephones seem to work for some people really well and for others much less so. I know in my early career I was always a little frightened of using the telephone … it always seems so intrusive as you don't know what the other person is doing when you call.

For a time, I didn't like calling people on the phone but with the advent of email and text my solution to overcome this was to text or email and ask when it was convenient for me to call. That allowed the other person to respond with a time that worked, and if they didn't respond; they weren't

---

[15] https://support.zoom.us/hc/en-us/articles/210707503-Virtual-Background

surprised when I did call. And as I said earlier ... ALWAYS ask if it's convenient once you are through to them!

More importantly, I believe, is once you are on the phone that you stay focussed and don't allow yourself to be distracted.

One technique I learnt years ago was to ...

Focus on an inanimate object when listening to someone talking to me on the phone. I find the best things are a door handle or a light switch. This stops me from getting distracted by looking at something out of the window or across the office.

Another way to stay focussed when on the phone is to write notes or repeat what the other person is saying in your head as you hear them say it. This has the added advantage of ensuring that you don't start thinking about what you are going to say next, rather than listening to the whole question or comment.

There is a video of me explaining this technique in the 'Step Out from The Shadows website'[16] providing more information on this. And remember that others can't see you nod or your expression so making the occasional "mmm" or "ah ha" as they speak will mean that they are aware that you are still listening.

Email or text

Email and text are really great tools ... but be careful not to rely on them. Humans are sociable beings and for most people, not having a personal

---

[16] www.stepoutfromtheshadows.co.uk

relationship with you will definitely mean the connection is weaker. A weaker connection can mean that when a problem occurs it is harder to fix.

Imagine you have a customer who is complaining about something that you or one of your team has done. If you have met them, chatted about things other than work and know a little about the way they like to communicate, it will be much easier to handle the problem than if you have only sent them letters.

You can't be as personal in writing …

It takes too long so you skip straight from "Hi" to business with rarely time for a, "how are you?"

Face to face you wouldn't walk into the room and say "Hello … let's get down to business". The small talk between the greeting and work is really important to help you build a connection.

If you use text or email for your personal conversations, make sure you don't slip into 'textspeak' at work. Emojis are more acceptable than they were but a note to the MD saying:

> *"Thanks for the email I will get back to you as soon as possible"*

written as:

> *"Tnx 4 the e-mail, I'll tell you l8r 👍👀"*

… isn't going to go down well!

This is a particular problem if you are responding on your phone.

I know I have put a "X" at the end of a work email and only realised with embarrassment as I pressed send!

Another thing to consider when writing is that the emphasis you give to a word may not be the emphasis that is read. Try reading the following sentence with the emphasis on the underlined word and see how the meaning changes.

I didn't say she stole my money.

I **didn't** say she stole my money.

I didn't **say** she stole my money.

I didn't say **she** stole my money.

I didn't say she **stole** my money.

I didn't say she stole **my** money.

I didn't say she stole my **money**.

Tone of voice, sarcasm and enthusiasm are just three things that get lost in the written word and you have no way to check the recipients' understanding. If you have a difficult message to deliver, whenever possible, speak to the other person and don't rely on email.

Actions you can take from this chapter:

- When contacting someone by phone or interrupting them ALWAYS ask if it is convenient.
- Stop what you are doing to really listen, focus on the other person or an inanimate object if on the phone.
- Have LUCID conversations - **L**isten to **U**nderstand, **C**larify and **I**nterpret and only then **D**iscuss.
- When on-line or video consider if the other person can see you, see anything you don't want them to see and if your hands are visible.
- Go to www.stepoutfromtheshadow.co.uk to see the video on how to really listen.
- Be careful not to use emojis or text-speak in your emails or messages
- Remember that emphasis and vocal tone can't be read. Speak to the other person if you want more than just the words to be understood.

CHAPTER 9

Presenting & storytelling

The time most people approach me with a real fear of stepping out from the shadows is when they have to present. This might be because you have to present to your colleagues, bosses and/or clients at work or you could now run your own business and are your own salesperson.

Let's face it, there aren't many roles these days when you don't have to present to someone, even if there is only one person in the audience. And I could (and many others have) write an entire book on how to improve your presentation skills. I have thought long and hard about what the most useful pointers are that I can provide in just a chapter.

All the elements that aid any communication that I have already talked about; eye contact, the smile, posture and the like, will help you look and sound more confident when presenting. As will looking the part. But you won't be the only one if you still sit somewhere between uncomfortable and terrified when presenting.

I liken confidence to a light switch in your head.

Sometimes it's a dimmer switch and fear slowly appears or disappears; it's something that you can control. More often though, it's like a flick switch where you suddenly feel the fear and your body reacts. Everyone has a switch in their head that flicks on in certain situations, and controlling this is much harder.

It might be that you are fine presenting to colleagues but your switch flicks when you are presenting to strangers … or vice versa.

Maybe it's the numbers in the audience … 3 is OK but not 30, 30 is OK but not 300. Maybe it's the purpose of the presentation … you're OK when delivering information but not if you think you are selling.

I remember talking to a client who headed up a division for a large company and was really comfortable speaking to his team. He talked about how he would get everyone (all 300 of them) into the warehouse and present standing on a pallet raised by a fork lift truck, so that everyone could see him.

Talking to 300 people didn't faze him. But ask him to present the budget to the board (a mere handful of people) and he was a gibbering wreck. The pressure of knowing that if the budget wasn't approved then he would have to lay people off, flicked his switch completely.

I spoke at the start of the book about what happens to our brains when we think we are in danger and what affect that has on our bodies. And if your switch flicks, the "Seven-Eleven" breathing technique I covered in Chapter 2 will help enormously.

But what else can you do?

Firstly, let's talk technology!

I'm old enough to remember when we didn't have PowerPoint, and speakers didn't use it as a crutch to lean on during their presentations. In fact, my first sales role entailed me turning up to a meeting with a machine the size of a microwave and heavier than a small child upon which I put a slide carousel. This was synchronised with a recording that gave a short overview of the business, barely audible over the clatter of slides dropping in and out!

So, you can imagine the excitement of many, myself included, when the joy of PowerPoint and ClipArt came our way. I and many others then bombarded our clients and colleagues with presentations created with multiple styles of transitions, multiple fonts and bullet points. Watching a presentation when it was all new was sometimes enough to set off a migraine in the audience.

Thankfully life has moved on but for many technology is still thought to be the start and end of every presentation. And it's not!

Remember that the reason people buy (whether you are selling a product, a service, an idea or a route forward) is because of you. They will base this decision on the way that you communicate and not on your skill at creating the slides for your presentation. So, consider delivering a presentation without a slide show. Use props and other visual aides if they add to your message but start off by putting 'you' front and centre stage.

If you have to use slides (and I know there are professions and companies where this is a requirement) then I would recommend the following:

When you start preparing your presentation don't start with the slides.

Work out what you want to say and HOW you are going to say it first. Think about where your will slow down or speed up. What will you emphasise? When will you get quieter to draw the audience in? How will you project your voice so you will be heard?

When you start to think about your visual aids, these should be the icing on the cake not the cake itself. If you can't deliver your presentation without the slides then go back to the brief and create it so you can.

Think about how you will cope if:

- there is a power cut,
- the leads to the projector don't work with your laptop,
- the power socket for your laptop is too far from where you are speaking and you can't change the slides from that position, or

- there is no projector and the room you are in feels like the longest ever built ... and you can't get near enough to your audience for them to see your computer screen[17].

Will you have to tell your audience that you can't do the presentation or will you be able to deliver your message anyway? If there was ever a confidence booster it was when I was the only person on the panel who could still deliver their presentation!

Remember that your slides, notes and handouts have different names ...

Because they're different things. Don't be tempted to create your slides as your notes. You will end up with far too many words ... and no-one wants to hear you reading the slide out loud.

Equally, printing out the slides isn't helpful for you during the presentation. The audience will end up reading ahead and not listening to you. If the slides make sense as a handout then use them for that and change your slides.

Finally, consider when you will use "Ctrl W" or "Ctrl B".

If you are using PowerPoint this will cause your screen to go blank and all eyes will move to you. There will be similar shortcuts on other software I'm sure ... or put in a blank slide which will work just as well.

If you rely on the slides alone then at best, the audience's memory of your presentation will merge into all the others they have sat through. At worst,

---

[17] All sound too far-fetched? These have all happened to me at different times since the advent of PowerPoint.

you will end up reading the slides out to your audience because you haven't thought about how you will deliver your message or practised your delivery.

Some of my clients have found the easiest way to move from creating slides to creating presentations is to think about the stories they can use to emphasise points and weave into the flow of the presentation.

As Philip Pullman is quoted as saying ...

"Thou shalt not is easily forgotten, once upon a time lasts forever".

So, whether you are creating a sales pitch or a team pep talk to get them on side, using stories will mean that your message is more likely to be remembered. If you can get your audience emotionally involved, they will remember the feeling and so remember what you said. If you just tell them information, they probably won't remember what you said, even tomorrow morning.

I have often been told that the topic is too difficult to create a story for or that a story will diminish the speaker's gravitas. I couldn't disagree more! A story makes even the most complicated information accessible and I have never seen a speaker lose their authority because they told a story. Just watch a few TED talks[18] and you will see what I mean.

The following are just a few ways that clients have transformed their presentations with stories:

You are selling a financial service ...
... so you create a character whose story emphasises
the problems that your customers have and how you

---

[18] www.ted.com

resolve them. The character is referenced throughout the presentation creating an ebb and flow for the audience to follow. So much better than giving a list of what you can do.

You are selling a pharmaceutical product …
… which only improves on your competitor's product by less than 0.5% but can be delivered in just one dose rather than their three. You tell the story of the impact of this from the patient's point of view rather than the physicians, thus forming an emotional link and changing the whole feeling of your presentation.

You are changing the structure of your business …
… which will mean major changes for your staff. You tell your story of what you wanted to create when you started the business. The staff understand what your motivation and journey was so they can understand the need of the changes. By the time you tell them what has to be done they are on-side and clear about your purpose.

If you tell stories it becomes easier to remember your own presentation so you need fewer notes – a mere word or picture will remind you of your next point. You will also find that your word choice and emphasis will change too.

Imagine you are the business owner I describe in my last example, changing the structure of your business and wanting to get your team on-board. Your enthusiasm and belief in the business when it was just you and your story will determine the vocabulary that you use.

As you can see the story unfold in your mind's eye …

So, you will describe what you are seeing and your emphasis will change. As you talk about the first £100 you earnt you will remember how you felt and that will come across in the way that you speak.

As you talk about your first pay cheque you will remember the pride you felt and you will sound proud. The audience will have context and something to compare against when you start to talk about the current situation you are in and why you are making these changes. They will be there with you.

And the real bonus of telling stories is that you will feel less nervous. Once you start talking and you are in the moment you will find all those "habits" like wandering feet, arm stroking and hair twisting will just disappear.

Everyone says a presentation needs a beginning, a middle and an end. I would add that each of these need a story that your audience will remember. Get it right and they will remember how you made them feel ... today, tomorrow and for years to come.

Actions you can take from this chapter:

- Use the "Seven-Eleven" breathing technique from Chapter 2 to help you in those moment when you switch 'flicks'.
- Consider not using PowerPoint or an equivalent for most presentations, if you must then make sure it is the icing on the cake, not the cake!
- Remember your slides, handouts and notes have different names because they should be different things.
- Put yourself front and centre as often as you can.
- Use stories to make your presentations easier to remember for you and more memorable for your audiences.

CHAPTER 10

A moment in your life

So, we are coming to the end of the book and I have covered the key areas of communication that I believe will make a difference to whether or not you are able to Step Out from The Shadows.

If you can quieten your inner voice, understand that others don't communicate in the same way as you do and adapt your communication style to suit them you will come a long way. Add to that, taking on board ways to make a great first impression, present yourself and be assertive when face to face, on the phone and even in your emails and you will start to move into the light.

I started this book with a moment in my life and now you are at a moment in yours. You picked up this book for a reason and if you have read the book all the way through then you are someone who wants to be able to stand up and speak out more often.

You don't want to stay on the side lines and hope you are noticed.

You want to take the opportunities that come your way and grab them with both hands.

You really do want to Step Out from The Shadows.

But reading a book isn't going to change much ... not on its own. If you are anything like me, you have bought books before, you have read books before and you have put them on your bookshelf before ... never to look at them again.

So, this is your chance to create a moment in your life that you can look back on. A moment when you made a decision to take a step to change your life.

Great communication is the basis of every relationship you have … the heart of relationship building. As my good friend and colleague Caroline Walker[19] (who works with teenage girls in building their confidence) put it …

> *Good communication leads us away from misunderstanding, conflict, waste of time and missed opportunities. And it leads us towards co-operation, collaboration, clarity, opportunities, positive working relationships, understanding, effectiveness, productivity, team working, strong leadership, solution-seeking, problem-solving and creativity.*

This isn't an exhaustive list and my intention throughout this book has been to show you why communication skills are so important. And what a difference you can make to every facet of your life by improving your understanding of how you like to communicate and how to adapt this to get the best outcome you can … for you and those you communicate with.

I'm a big believer in setting goals and aspiring to get ahead, but setting goals without a plan of action is like writing a letter to Father Christmas as a young child and hiding it somewhere safe. If you never tell a grown up what you want then your wishes are likely to stay wishes. And if you don't do something to achieve your goals … they will just stay wishes too.

You have to take action.

Taking a step towards a goal is always a better decision than just thinking about it. I've been thinking about writing this book for several years but it wasn't until I started telling people, creating a plan of action and doing something that the book began to materialise.

---

[19] https://www.confidentteens.co.uk/

So, what do you do next? Well firstly I hope you won't put this book on the bookshelf and forget about it! I've designed it so you can dip in and out over the months ahead.

Kolb's learning model[20] published in 1984 shows the way that you experience learning.

Put at its simplest to really take information on board ...

- You think about doing something (plan),
- you take action (do it),
- you reflect on how it went (review) and then
- decide on what/if you need to do something different to get a better outcome (adapt).

---

[20] https://en.wikipedia.org/wiki/Kolb%27s_experiential_learning

What most of us forget is to review and adapt after we've taken action.

So, as well as planning a route to your goal you need to revisit what you have done, to check it is still getting you where you want and to see if you need to adapt what you are doing.

All too often I meet people who have tried a new technique or approach and when it doesn't work decide that it's not for them. As my Granny used to say … "If at first you don't succeed; try, try again". But I would add "having first reviewed what you did and what you need to change"!

Each chapter topic could have been a book in itself and what I have done here is give you a few tips and techniques to help you make some changes but if you would like to know more then go to the Step Out from The Shadows website[21].

The free information I have referred to throughout the book is there for you to watch and download and if you want to carry on your journey into the spotlight then I tell you how to do that there too.

You can already communicate …

And it's very unlikely that everything I have written here will be new to you. And you don't want to just start doing new things. There may be habits that no longer serve you so I have included on the website a template we use in some of our workshops to help our delegates reflect on what they have learnt.

It's a sheet that helps you to consider what you have learnt and what you are going to do with that learning. What you will stop doing, what you will

---

[21] http://www.stepoutfromtheshadows.co.uk/

start doing and (because you will be doing some of this already) what you will continue doing.

Remember that communication isn't something you work on and forget. It is something that needs constant work. People change, the tools we use to communicate change and our circumstances, roles and thoughts change too.

What else can you do?

A lot of the techniques I have covered are pretty easy to implement but you don't have to do them all at the same time. I would just pick one area that you want to improve on, pick a couple of actions and work on them for a week or two.

Then take 10 minutes to review how the changes have gone. Has it been easy? Are there things you would do differently next time? How can you improve on the outcome?

If you have any questions, I have set up a way for you to get your questions answered on the website and I would love your feedback so please take the opportunity to speak to me!

Go to the website[22] and register there for the Q&A session. I have some great plans to help you stay accountable to yourself and carry on developing your communication skills.

Take this moment in your life to decide that you are going to Step Out from The Shadows. Do it alone, work with a friend to improve together or go to the website and work with me.

---

[22] http://www.stepoutfromtheshadows.co.uk/

Whatever you do, take action ...

... and move one step further out from the shadows.

About the Author

With a degree in Psychology & Drama and a Diploma in Management, Sally has spent much of her career in sales and client service roles. She has witnessed first-hand how poor communication can make or break a deal, a relationship or a business. Clients buy from who they like best, staff work late because of who asks them and colleagues work better with some individuals than others.

Since 2000, Sally has run 'Partners With You Ltd', a company that uses the skills of professional actors to help business people communicate more effectively and confidently on any stage or in front of camera.

'Partners With You' provides both in-house and open workshops around presentation skills, storytelling, team building. And it delivers impact & influence programmes for large blue-chip clients as well as small business/ individuals looking for personal development.

Believing in continuous development, Sally has trained as an Enterprise and Career Mentor, an accredited Wellness coach and PRISM Brain Mapping practitioner. She combines her personal skills to mentor individuals and runs workshops on key topics to help you to 'step out from the shadows'.

Sally is a contributor to Steve Bridger's book **Transform Your Communication Skills** and writes a regular column for The Watford Observer and other Newsquest local papers.

Step Out from the Shadows is Sally's first book.